Elisabeth Stevens

The Night Lover

The Night Lover

Elisabeth Stevens

BIRCH
BROOK
PRESS

First edition
Library of Congress Catalog Number: 94-072882
ISBN: 0-913559-26-1

Etchings by the author, Elisabeth Stevens

Several poems in *The Night Lover* are forthcoming in
The Maryland Poetry Review and *Late Knocking*.

Typeset and printed letterpress at

Birch Brook Press

PO Box 81

Delhi, NY 13753

Write for free catalog of books and art.

The author wishes to thank The Ragdale Foundation,
The Virginia Center for the Creative Arts and Yaddo,
where some of these poems were written.

To H.R.R.

CONTENTS

I. The Year Begins

13/SONG
15/FEBRUARY FOUR A.M.
17/SPRING EQUINOX
19/MONDAY MORNING

II. Summer

25/A WAVE CAME
26/I WROTE YOU A LETTER
27/EMERGENCY
28/I DIDN'T WANT HER IN MY GARDEN
30/I MISS YOUR BODY
31/I SAW THE MOON RISE
32/SWIMMING TO THE DAM
34/I SAW AN OCEAN LINER IN THE CHANNEL
35/VISION
36/I WENT FOR A WALK LAST NIGHT
37/YOU INHABIT MY MIND

III. The Year Wanes

43/AFTER THE FINAL FIRE
44/PRESENCE
45/VOYAGE TO THE OTHER SHORE
46/GREY WINTER TREES
47/JOURNEY TO THE NEW YEAR

IV. Ever After

53/CONSTELLATION

I. The Year Begins

SONG

When the moon has come down to the frost line,
when cold stars have drowned in the sea,
The Night Lover approaches:
he spans the sky for me.

In the room where I am sleeping,
my hands crossed on my breast,
I dream he is lying beside me—
when I awake, he is.

I do not raise my eyelids,
I do not breathe his name:
I open my flesh to his body,
his flesh is chilled, then warm.

At daybreak when I'm still sleeping,
he's gone without a word.
There's a dent in the pillow beside me,
a lingering perfume in the bed.

All day long in the sunlight,
I sleepwalk through ought and should
while waiting, waiting for evening
when shadows advance from the wood.

The hour of moonrise approaches,
then the time of his broad-winged return.
The Night Lover of dreams and darkness
will rock me to sleep in his arms.

For him I will hold back the sunrise,
for him I will rise with the winds:
we will ride to the West together,
to the West—where the night never ends.

FEBRUARY FOUR A.M.

Through the night crack
in the winter window,
a spume of fog
spirals toward the bed.

It expands
through coils of the springs,
dampens the mattress,
seeps between the sheets.

Soon
we lie on a white sea,
merge like clouds.
Mist rises around us.

I am not afraid,
I am in your arms.
Together we float
as the fog tide rises.

How can it be?
We glide through the window,
circle softening snow piles,
icy tips of pines.

Where are we going?
Down the quiet street,
beyond the lamplight,
to the forest, the hills, the shore.

Wherever fog carries us
we will be there together,
our bodies relaxed, transparent,
white as shades, whiter than mist.

There is a lassitude,
a lack of definition.
We merge with the fog
that transforms us.

Part of it,
part of each other,
part of others forever gone.

SPRING EQUINOX

Warm, unseasonable dampness
undulates through

transparent white curtains stiffened
by winter grime.

I hear a faint, persistent tap-tap—
early wings in a lampshade.

Silence . . .
nothing moves.

I lie across the foot of the bed
naked, covers thrown back.

You enter the room,
a moist edge of a wool blanket

scratches my thighs.
Roots of my hair itch.

Humidity fuels aggravation,
forces its way between us.

It smells like pale brown gas
mixed with dark brown dust.

It feels like coarse-grained sand
trickling between my legs.

I cannot get up till the weather changes.
At the equinox, I cannot breathe.

MONDAY MORNING

You go sullen, unsmiling,
not a word.

After moon rings—white sugar doughnuts—
I want you,

but your bag of dreams is shut.
I slam the door on your footsteps.

Then, as your nectar evaporates,
I cry in sugar-moistened sheets.

II. Summer

A WAVE CAME

When we swam far out,
laughed at the undertow, embraced,
a wave came.

I grasped for you—
you were torn from me—
when the wave came.

I heard you cry
far away in foam,
but the wave drew me down

dark undertow fathoms
to green seaweed silence.
When the wave spewed me up

I saw the sun, the moon,
the cloudless sky, the endless ripples,
and the white, blinding mirror
of an empty, horizonless sea.

I WROTE YOU A LETTER

I wrote you a letter,
wanted to give it to you.

You wouldn't come for it.
I went to the post office,

sent it registered.
I imagined that letter

turned to a wall of glass,
even a sheet of steel

rising on your bed
between you and her.

EMERGENCY

I sirened to your house at midnight,
blood in my mouth, salt in my eyes.
Nobody home.

I waited patiently at the front walk,
gazed down the hill at the city hospital,
its orange lights.

I heard you behind me,
hurrying home.
Your face was white as a gauze bandage.

The operation was over in seconds.
You twisted your key like a scalpel,
shut the door in my face.

I DIDN'T WANT HER IN MY GARDEN

I wrote you,
I begged you,
I didn't want her in my garden.

The gate is open.
I suspect you brought her
last night

when I wasn't home.
Did she pass my hollyhocks—
red and yellow sentinels?

Did she breach my hedges—
olives that you helped me plant
our first fall long ago?

Did she sear past soft leaves
of my star magnolia—
her orange hair flaming?

I think she withered
white floribundas—thorny roses meant
to guard the window set down low.

I am sure you saw her
strip the daisies' petals
with her purple nails.

I can see you standing
poised at the overlook
like a cold cenotaph,

a stone phallus, a sharpened pike,
while she wasted everything,
spreading pests and poisons,

on that no moon midnight
I went to another bed
and wasn't coming home.

I MISS YOUR BODY

I miss your body.
I miss nightlong journeys
from your mouth
to your genitals,

territory
I explored,
declivities and projections
I knew well.

If you would only
take my head
between your palms,
pause,

pull a hair
from clotted lips,
bite them
so blood runs free.

You won't speak
or write.
I don't want words—
I want your body.

I SAW THE MOON RISE

I saw the moon rise
behind dark trees
overlooking dark water.

The moon was almost full
and ringed
with a halo of light.

I saw your shadow
rise from the shoreline,
higher than the pines.

(Were you standing at sunset
on the horizon
miles behind me?)

I saw your arms open,
your fingers spread.
I rose to your moon-pale greyness,
I was absorbed.

SWIMMING TO THE DAM

The day I swam to the dam,
I didn't want to drown,
I wanted to say good-bye.

Alone in the opaque pond,
trees bent over its banks
like green angels,

I was weighed down
as though carrying your body
in my arms.

I made it the whole way,
touched the moss-shrouded wall,
let the water take everything.

I turned,
saw an enormous weed
growing beside the sluiceway.

With a quick breath,
I started back,
light and easy.

A long way, but
I was not tired.
Almost there,

sure of myself,
I called back:
"Good-bye, *good-bye.*"

From the sluiceway,
came the echo:
"Good-bye, good . . . bye. . . ."

I SAW AN OCEAN LINER IN THE CHANNEL

I saw an ocean liner in the channel.
It was an illusion of moonrise,
a midsummer fantasy.

I saw the prow, the decks, the smokestacks,
imagined it was our cruiser
to distant islands.

I knew then I would take your hands again,
our journey together
was not over.

VISION

I am on one shore,
you on the other.

A great flight of grey birds
rises between us, circles south.

The end of day, the end of August,
the end of summer.

Sundown tide, thick as blood,
ebbs out.

Somewhere someone is dying.
Somewhere something is born.

I WENT FOR A WALK LAST NIGHT

I went for a walk last night.
The half moon was September yellow,
the lighted windows shrouded by screens.

Coming back by my hollyhocks,
I sensed you,
waiting behind the star magnolia.

In the dimness,
I saw your crossed arms,
called your name.

You were pale as Lazarus.
I stretched out my hand—
your flesh was cold.

We kissed.
Your face, like the moon,
was half-hidden.

Your mouth was hard,
your hands rough as sand,
your tongue strong as tides.

YOU INHABIT MY MIND

You inhabit my mind
as though straddling my legs,
then kneeling
to descend to my thighs.

You enter my thoughts
unexpectedly, penetrate
cerebral convolutions, hidden fissures,
red moons, black tides.

You crack my eggshell skull,
suck secrets.
My eyes glaze, my arms clasp,
I writhe through clouds, winds, mists, willows—
my mouth open, my hair streaming, my legs spread wide.

III. The Year Wanes

AFTER THE FINAL FIRE

After the final cookout fire
in October—a warm day out of season—
we are on the terrace after dinner at twilight
under a blue smoke sky, a single star.
You, love, sleep as the cat prowls your lap.
Silence, only a single cricket.
Everything is warm and calm and still,
the shadow of the star magnolia
advances across the slates.

While you breathe heavily,
your chest rises and falls, rises and falls,
I feel them come from nowhere, move around us—
the recent dead, the long dead. It makes no difference—
their space is no thicker than a sheet of paper.
We are their players, they, our silent audience.
For now. Until, with the turn of a wheel,
the creak of a wheel chair, the fall of a hair,
we shall be among them.

PRESENCE

You extend beyond yourself
like a sea pool at full moon,
like wind swelled by storms.

You are more than flesh and shadow,
more than breath and voice,
a presence sensed—not seen.

Before you knock, I open,
before you ask, I answer,
before you touch I feel your fingers—

Here.

VOYAGE TO THE OTHER SHORE

We went to the other shore today—
last voyage of the season.

Going over took two hours,
coming back—more.

Over there, currents were against us,
winds wrong from the north.

Coming back was easy—indolent.
We floated, it seemed, on glass.

Two container ships crossed our course—
grey shadows against the glare.

We slowed, let them pass to sea.
The engine did not falter.

Back at the dock—another afternoon gone—
the sun was setting.

It could have been days, even years,
since we had left our moorings.

The chill, slanting light
changed everything.

We had come a long way.
We would go further—
when winter had come and gone.

GREY WINTER TREES

Grey winter trees
in grey-brown fog
seen between
half-parted curtains. . . .

Dun-colored birds
visible until
they rise above the sash
into snow-weighted sky.

The room is cold,
the air is damp.
Your mouth is
wet.

JOURNEY TO THE NEW YEAR

"We will be driving all night."
"I know that."
After a warm bed, an embrace,
we are in your dank yard by the hill above the tracks.

Through the icy mist, a train whistle cries.
You slam car doors.
We turn up the alley,
pass someone, head down.

"Is that your son?" I ask.
"It looks like him."
"Where is he going?"
"The other way."

You drive on,
take the back road to the highway.
We pass rows of quiet houses,
smiling Santas, blinking Christmas lights.

We are the only car,
then we turn into six lane traffic.
The insides of my ears itch. I inch down a window.
Dampness enters. We go faster.

It is a long way to the ocean.
When we get there, we will see the sunrise,
hear the whitecaps, smell the sand.
The old year will be behind us.

Our boat waits, strains at its moorings.
We sail early, out of the harbor.
We will leave the city behind.
We have begun a long journey.

We are not coming back.

IV. Ever After

CONSTELLATION

Far into the night sky
we travel past planets
clutching each other
until blood congeals.

Our thighs, our arms
even the gentle swellings
of our eyelids and
the half moons of our nails

are like white marble—
cold, smooth.
Stone to night's hammer,
we break, we shatter.

Our paroxyms are
explosive, icy,
brilliant, blinding—
we are stars.

We are dispersed.
We are fragments
whose positions will be traced
from hilltops by astronomers.

We have been transformed
into a constellation—
The Lovers—the pale, flickering reflection
of two figures, forever clasped.

Breast to breast, arms interlocked,
legs intertwined,
our eyes are lights to sail by,
our loins a single lamp.

We have transcended
our earthly outlines.
We will shine
shine, shine, shine.

THE AUTHOR/ARTIST

A fiction writer, poet and journalist, Elisabeth Stevens is the author of six books. Her collections of short fiction are: *Horse and Cart: Stories From the Country*, Wineberry Press, 1990; *Fire & Water: Six Stories*, Perivale Press, 1983; and *The Towers*, Signal Books, 1995. Her poetry collections are: *Children of Dust: Portraits & Preludes*, The New Poets Series, 1985; and *The Night Lover*, Birch Brook Press, 1995. *Elisabeth Stevens' Guide to Baltimore's Inner Harbor* was published by Stemmer House in 1981. A resident of Baltimore, Ms. Stevens is the winner of fiction awards from *The Maryland Poetry Review* and *Lite Circle*, and a drama award from The Baltimore Writers Alliance.

As a journalist, she has written many articles, art reviews and book reviews. She is a former art critic of *The Washington Post*, *The Wall Street Journal*, *The Trenton Times* and, most recently, *The Baltimore Sun*.

THE BOOK

was set by hand in 12 pt. Deepdene, a font designed by Frederic W. Goudy. It was printed letterpress on 80 lb. Mohawk Vellum, cream white, with Superior's Black Marvel ink. Cover stock is Tomohawk.